THE NEW EDUCATION:

...L) TRAINING AN INDISPENSABLE DEPARTMENT OF IT.

AN ESSAY

IN EXPLANATION OF THE

Gramercy Park School and Tool-house

SITUATED AT

104 EAST 20th STREET, NEW YORK,

(REAR OF ALL-SOULS' CHURCH,)

BY COURTLANDT PALMER.

ISSUED FROM
THE PRINTING DEPARTMENT OF THE INSTITUTE.
1885.

THE NEW EDUCATION:

MANUAL (INDUSTRIAL) TRAINING AN INDISPENSABLE DEPARTMENT OF IT.

AN ESSAY

IN EXPLANATION OF THE

Gramercy Park School and Tool-house

SITUATED AT

104 EAST 20th STREET, NEW YORK,

(REAR OF ALL-SOULS' CHURCH,)

BY COURTLANDT PALMER.

ISSUED FROM
THE PRINTING DEPARTMENT OF THE INSTITUTE.
1885.

Prefatory Notice.

This essay was read on recurring Thursday evenings before successive audiences, in response to the following request from the eminent citizens, clergymen and educators, whose names are subjoined:

Courtlandt Palmer, Esq.

Dear Sir :

Knowing that you regard the Gramercy Park School and Tool-house as a great improvement in educational methods, we respectfully request of you to deliver an address explanatory of its objects and advantages.

F. A. P. Barnard,
C. F. Chandler,
Parke Godwin,
G. Gottheil,
Andrew Carnegie,
Abram S. Hewitt,
E. L. Youmans,
R. Heber Newton,
William Lloyd,
F. B. Thurber.
G. von Taube.

On one of these occasions the reading was listened to by President Andrew D. White, of Cornell University. A few days later he kindly wrote the following letter, which he permits to be published :

President's Rooms,
Cornell University.

Ithica, N. Y., *March 28th*, 1885.

My dear sir :

Allow me to say that I was greatly impressed by your recent lecture upon the instruction in the mechanic arts as connected with ordinary school training, as well as by the subjects naturally related thereto which you then touched upon. I have long believed that schools such as you have been endeavoring to establish are among the greatest necessities of this country. There is too much training of men to get a living by their wits, and not enough to enable them to get a living by their hands. I earnestly hope for your success in New York, and believe that your lecture ought to be brought before audiences of thinking people in various parts of the country. I should be very glad, if it be consistent with your other duties, if you could come here and deliver it before our students. Your doing so would be a philanthropic work, and could hardly fail to produce admirable results, since our young men go out into all parts of the country, and are, doubtless, to take influential places in the communities to which they shall go—many of them in State, and some of them, perhaps, in National councils.

I remain, dear sir,
Very truly yours,
ANDREW D. WHITE.

Courtlandt Palmer, Esq.,
117 E. 21st St., New York.

THE NEW EDUCATION:

MANUAL (INDUSTRIAL) TRAINING

AN INDISPENSABLE DEPARTMENT OF IT.

The hope of the future lies in Education. It is hard to teach old dogs new tricks, but just as true now as when it was written is the ancient text: "Train up a child in the way he should go, and when he is old he will not depart from it."

My object in this paper is to lay before you, in its general outline, the scheme of the Gramercy Park School, and the Tool-house as an essential portion of its curriculum.

What I shall have to say is largely adapted, in part from Herbert Spencer's celebrated work on Education, but mostly from notes of conversations held with Mr. G. von Taube, the principal of the school under consideration. There is, therefore, but little of my own original thought in this paper, my object being not to indite a new and brilliant essay, but merely to present the most recent learning upon this most important subject as best I may. Thus I have not hesitated to interweave from both of the authorities I have referred to not only their thoughts, but often their actual words.

The following anecdote seems to me to represent not inaptly the old educational methods. It is told of John Randolph and Tristram Burgess, who were formerly both representatives at our National Capitol from their respective States of Virginia and Rhode Island. The two, it is said, were walking together one day along Pennsylvania Avenue, when they chanced to meet a drove of donkeys. "Behold your constituents!" said the supercilious Southerner, pointing to the animals. "Yes," retaliated the Yankee, "I see they are headed South, to teach the young Virginians." And better, perhaps, such teaching than much which we have undergone. Well do I remember, and sadly do I recall, my school experiences of younger days. A false and arbitrary culture of the mind, in entire disregard of any well-considered system either of pedagogics or of ethics, was then the sole solicitude. School-hours were wearisomely protracted, and the stuffing of dry knowledge, pretty much as ammunition and wadding are rammed into a gun, was deemed the one thing needful.

In place of a harmonious and growthful development of body and brain, there was substituted an artificial and mechanical drilling, enforced by the rod of the petty pedagogue, whose object was by a sort of battering ram process, *to knock the old Adam out and knock knowledge in.*

A régime of rote-learning was thus instituted—a régime involving parrot-like recitations of almost unintelligible rules and formulas—a mere empty twittering, as it were, which conveyed to the learner's mind not facts, but the empty symbols of facts; that is to say, in the language of Hamlet, nothing but "words, words, words."

And what was aimed at? Not the development, but the decoration of the mind; not the forming of stable characters, but the production of striking impressions, just as voyagers uniformly find that colored beads and trinkets are much more prized by wild tribes, than are the really useful calicos or broad-cloths. It is safe to say that, under the old régime, the most necessary training was that to which the least time was given. We know, for example, that for such a common craft as shoemaking, a long course of close apprenticeship is deemed desirable; but boys might enter life, with its varied pursuits, its enormous activities, and its urgent needs, fortified with little more than a course of Latin and Greek—which was applied afterwards to no practical purposes—and girls might find their preparation for motherhood and the home in a smattering of music, poetry and the foreign languages.

There cannot fail, however, to be a close relationship between any system of education and the social state with which it coexists, and these olden methods, which I am criticising, with all their superficiality and petty tyranny, have come down to us from the arbitrary conditions of the past, both in government and in society.

Under such conditions, as they prevailed less than a century ago, along with political discipline, stern in its commands, ruling by force of terror, visiting trifling crimes with death, and implacable in its vengeance on the disloyal, there necessarily grew up an academic discipline similarly harsh; a discipline of multiplied injunctions and blows for every breach of them; a discipline of unlimited autocracy, upheld by the ferule and the black hole.

But "old things are passing away; behold, old things are becoming new." The decline of *authority*, whether papal, philosophic, kingly or pedagogic, is essentially one phenomenon, and in all these domains the republic has succeeded to monarchy as the destiny of man. To fit human beings for republicanism, self-reliant citizens must be evolved. Thus, despotic sway from without having been largely removed in the realm of the State, arbitrary dogmatism must correspondingly disappear from the school, so that children may grow up not to depend upon external law, but to be a law unto themselves. The government from without must be supplanted by the rule from within; command must give way to character; culture must come to overweigh mere accomplishments, so-called.

Thus comes the question of questions, to wit: how to determine (to use a phrase of Bacon's) the relative value of *knowledges*. In other words, is there any criterion amid the conflicting claims of the various studies by which we may be guided? "Yes," quickly the answer comes, "there is, viz.: Human Welfare, Human Happiness. How to live, in the widest sense; how to treat body and mind; how to manage our affairs; how to bring up a family; how to behave as a citizen; how to use all our faculties for ourselves and others; how to live completely; these are the real functions of a true education."

To such an end a classification of the leading *activities* becomes essential. Such activities thus arrange themselves in the order of their relative importance:

1. Those which minister directly to self-preservation.

2. Those which, by securing the necessities of life, minister *indirectly* to self-preservation.

3. Those which have for their end the rearing and discipline of offspring.

4. Those which are involved in the maintenance of proper social and political relations.

5. Those miscellaneous activities which make up the leisure part of life, gratifying the tastes and feelings.

Such, at least, is Herbert Spencer's able and valuable classification, but for my purpose, in order from my point of view to treat the subject clearly, perhaps no arrangement of the topic can be better than its natural division into *physical*, *intellectual* and *moral education*. Let us rapidly review these three domains.

FIRST.—PHYSICAL EDUCATION.

This I shall be compelled to pass over (from want of time) with scarcely more than a single remark. The primal necessity of life is to be a good animal. A sound body must be taken as the desirable basis of a sound mind, and also of a clear conscience.

This is thoroughly appreciated in the Gramercy Park School, where open-air exercises in the square, and indoor exercises in the gymnasium, are amply provided, its whole system of physical development being based upon a thorough acquaintance with physiology and hygiene.

SECOND.—INTELLECTUAL EDUCATION.

Recent psychological (or mental physiological) science has brought to us, perhaps, the greatest of all modern discoveries—the existence, that is, of a strict correlation between the brain and nervous system on the one hand, and thought, with its workings, on the other.

With this clue in hand, educational methods may now follow an established line of mental facts, based on actual physiological laws. These I shall touch upon more fully as I proceed, but for the present state them categorically as follows :

a.—The development of the senses in the young is the basis of their future mentality.

b.—Such development, to be successful, necessitates individual work by the pupil, instead of rote-teaching and book-learning.

c.—Commemoration is based not on direct verbal drilling of the memory, but upon the association of impressions, conducting thence to the association of ideas.

d.—Ideas presuppose facts, and are the results drawn from comparisons of perceptions, depending, therefore, for their clearness, upon the quality of the perceptions which are obtained.

If we are willing to grant that the phenomena of intelligence conforms to such laws; if we are ready to admit that the evolution of intelligence in a child also conforms to such laws, it follows inevitably that education can be rightly guided only by a knowledge of these laws. And it furthermore follows that such education, depending thus on *things* instead of *words*, is of necessity from the *particular* to the *general*, from the *concrete* to the *abstract*, and from the *simple* to the *complex*.

But utterly regardless of every one of these palpable truths, highly complicated and abstract subjects, such as algebra and grammar, are frequently put at an early age into the hands of the unfortunate child. And, generally speaking, whilst the right class of facts is continually withheld, the wrong class is forcibly administered in the wrong way, and in the wrong order. Not recognizing that the function of books is supplementary, primers are thrust into the hands of the little ones years too soon, to their great injury. Not till a child's restless *observation* has been diligently cultivated should books be largely given to him, since the *words* in a book can be rightly interpreted into *ideas* only in proportion to the antecedent experience of *things*. And in this process the pupil should be taught by his teacher as little as possible, and should teach himself as much as possible. He, consequently, should be encouraged to work his own way, the self-made child thus leading on to the self-made man. Having done this, and having, by the doing of it, assimilated and organized his knowledge as he goes along, the learner finds himself ever coming into the possession of fresh agencies, which stand ready at hand to help him on towards the solution of all new cases as they arise.

With this end in view, that is to say, the learning of things instead of words, the most important new practice undoubtedly is, as already hinted, the systematic culture of the powers of observation. Some one has well said in this connection: "The education of the senses neglected, all after-education partakes of a drowsiness, a haziness, an insufficiency, which it is impossible to cure." In other words, ignoring nature and the natural, a vague, artificial ideal has been aimed at, bringing as its inevitable result a general dissatisfaction.

Hence, as the only alternative, the necessity of object-lessons, or a return to the concrete, which carries a child's mind through the same process that the mind of humanity at large has gone through; for instance, as in the truths of number, form and position, all of which, originally, were drawn by the race from actual objects.

This general reference to object-teaching now enables me to pass from Herbert Spencer, whom thus far I have been extensively quoting, to the authority of Mr. von Taube himself. He claims that the first bright light which came to illumine the dark labyrinth of educational theory, shot from the warm heart and brilliant mind of the Swiss teacher, Pestalozzi.

This reformer laid down the postulate that ideas are the result of sensations; that sensations arise from perceptions; that perceptions are dependent on the powers and possibilities of our sensory organs; that these organs can be cultivated, and that, consequently, perceptions and sensations can be quickened and improved. This theory has since been further developed and scientifically elaborated by Bain, Maudsley, Carpenter, Youmans, and others. It may be said, moreover, that to the researches of such savans is due the credit of having affirmed the invaluable truth that there is a certain *sequence*, in which the faculties spontaneously develop, and that, as a consequence, a properly adapted kind of knowledge is necessary for each step of the succession.

But the German Frœbel, the founder of the Kindergarten, was the one to whom is due not only the honor of having systematized, as a mere theory, the somewhat shadowy ideas of Pestalozzi (by bringing them into harmony with the facts of mental physiology), but to him also is to be accorded the lofty praise of having practically applied such theory to the real requirements of early instruction. If Pestalozzi recognized the human mind as subject only to a gradual development—a matter which had been, in truth, in a crude way, always understood—Frœbel was he who earliest informed the world when and how such development takes place. Thus we have, at last, been enabled to classify school existence physiologically, as presenting different states or ages of mental growth, and therefore of mental capacity.

At birth, the average weight of a healthy brain is from twelve to thirteen ounces, which, from the earliest childhood, up to six or seven years of age, increases to an average of forty ounces. During this period, and as related to this phenomenon, we now know the human mind to be possessed of an incomparable freshness for perceptions of the *concrete*.

The next stage of a child's development would bring him to thirteen or fourteen. In this interim, the brain-growth, though slower, adds to itself about five ounces more, and related to this, again, the pupil manifests the characteristics of curiosity and of natural propensity to *investigate* his surroundings. From fourteen to seventeen or nineteen we find a well-pronounced capacity for the recognition of similarities and differences between the *items* and *parts* observed. From that age to twenty-one or twenty-three, some three ounces only of extra brain-tissue are accumulated. A certain callousness of receptivity as to mere facts is then easily distinguishable; but in lieu thereof, the comparison of *ideas*, the solution of difficult problems, strong opinions and severe judgments, become pronounced characteristics, gradually toned down and modified by the more mature experiences of after life, when hardly any further change in the weight of the brain becomes perceptible.

The first two of these stages represent the *absorptive* capacity of the human mind from without, and the two later ones the inner systematization and working out of the materials thus previously gathered. How to select these materials for the first two stages—that has been the problem; the human mind—even the plastic mind of youth—having only, at most, a limited capacity for details. Such mental limitations being the case, children, it is claimed, should have offered to them not empty words and arid formulas; not fairy tales, fantastic poems, and graphic descriptions—immersing them in an ocean of false fancy and emotionalism—but they should be provided with the foundation stones (bright jewels they are) of those sciences, the understanding of which conditions our existence, and which, if only properly presented, the young will drink in with as much avidity and pleasure as they will the Arabian Nights, especially as the difficulties encountered by older people in mastering *minutiæ* do not exist in anything like the same degree for children. The reason of this is self-evident, when it is asserted that there is no science which does not start with things familiar even to the child. All problems, moreover, be it understood, are vastly simplified, even for the children themselves, by the facility with which every branch of knowledge can now be analyzed and reduced to a few fundamental propositions; which propositions, in turn, are based on a few fundamental facts. These facts, with their related propositions, once thoroughly mastered, the child straightway comes into the possession of the framework of his future knowledge.

Guided by this idea, there are given in the school-system under consideration, gradually developing lessons in plants, animals, and place—the foundations of a future knowledge of botany, geology, and geography; oral lessons in language, including qualities and names of objects, etc., etc.; lessons in reading, attention being drawn to thoughts rather than to words, and including, in time, proper poetic selections and historical and biographical sketches; lessons in writing, the pupil later on attempting to describe, in his own words, the objects learned from the oral lessons in the shape of compositions on clothing, cotton, linen, silk, etc., etc., the A B C of future technology; lessons in form, size, and number, leading on to arithmetic and solid measure; lessons in æsthetics, beginning with objective outlines of familiar things, triangles, quadrangles, etc., etc., etc., coming, later on, to curves and figures drawn from memory, and finally, to rudiments of the human figure and perspective, forming, thuswise, the elements of that technique in art, without which art degenerates into a vague emotionalism.

So, in very brief outline, pass the first two stages, comprising six years, which together constitute the objective course.

Next come the second two stages, which make up the subjective course, and which relate to ideas rather than to things—ideas, it is claimed, resulting from comparisons of perceptions in their similarities, differences, and oppositions, as, *e. g.*, hot as against cold, black as against white, night as against day. These subjective stages are, therefore, more purely intellectual.

The full development of the pupil's capabilities in these latter periods depends, however, upon the successful gathering of material during the previous objective courses; still, as remarked, it is the *idea*, and not the *thing* producing the idea, which, for the first time, becomes the important factor. A new instrument of criticism in this second or subjective division is now introduced, viz.: logical argument. Every idea is taken as a symbol of a previously learned fact. A definition is obtained, representing the summing up of previous concrete experiments; in other words, "correct thinking" is approached; ("correct thinking," as regulated by things;) "correct thinking," which has frequently been suggested as the best definition of Education; but if so, it must be understood as meaning the outcome of a previous training, the smooth run, as it were, of our mental mechanism, presupposing all parts of the same to be previously not only well oiled, but also well fitted together. Having collected the raw material, *i. e.*, the objective, it is not only our duty, but our necessity, to fit it and oil it before we can attempt to study the activity of the mechanism itself, *i.e.*, the subjective.

In this connection, furthermore, it seems to me not amiss to allude to the cultivation of the memory afforded by the process under consideration. The cultivation of the memory it is, which, *par excellence*, is claimed as the peculiar glory of the old method, but I do not hesitate to assert that if it did develop this faculty, it did so only in a mechanical, artificial, and factitious way. As against this erroneous result, true memory would now be cultivated in the manner nature itself suggests—through the *association of ideas.* The ability to repeat the Illiad of Homer, for example, indicates little more than a dead capacity of merely verbal power; but connections of ideas should correspond not simply to *words*, but to facts in their causal relations; such connections of ideas should remain the compound acquisition obtained, not alone through the hearing, but through the aid of all the senses; they should exercise not only the strength of recollection, but of understanding also, and should strengthen the memory *through* the understanding.

The whole method, in its *ensemble*, is readily seen to be based upon simple common sense, when we say that it is the relation between cause and consequence, whether among things or thoughts, enabling us in the end, through general propositions, to draw deductions, and so to arrive at and to meet special cases.

Such being the philosophical explanation or theory of the two latter, or subjective stages, let us now see what they actually embrace. In science, forces tend to take the place of facts; the mechanical principles involved in physiology are dwelt upon; biology, leading to mental and moral science, are in time approached; logic, inductive and deductive, comes towards the end, and political economy is embraced; in language, higher readings; and in writing, more complex compositions follow upon industrial, scientific, historical, social, sociological, and artistic topics; in mathematics, higher arithmetic is brought in, leading on to book-keeping, algebra, trigonometry, surveying and astronomy; in æsthetics, comes the gradual introduction of colors, also the theory of shades in drawing, and skeleton sketching from nature; and finally philosophy is brought in as manifested in its principal systems, Greek, French, German and English, involving a training in the evolution of human thought, together with a review of the most famous literatures of all nations.

Such, in a rapid sketch, constitute the materials of the second half of the school-course, comprising the two subjective stages, and occupying in all six years; the total course, both objective and subjective, thus consuming twelve; and, I may add, that throughout the whole curriculum, the modern, and, if desired, the ancient languages, are taught according to nature's methods.

It behooves us now to examine what incentives are best calculated to stimulate application and interest in the scholars, especially in the little ones. Here, again, care is needed, in our judgment. Persuasion and logical argument have been found by experience to be of but little avail. To work for love or fear of mamma and papa—as most of us parents must, in honesty, confess—partakes largely of the peculiarity of dissolving views. *Punishments*, on the other hand, can only be considered in the light of calamities. They are the first and strongest impressions stamped upon the budding reason of the child, inevitably leading him to detest an occupation associated with so much suffering. It is impossible to inflict misery except at the price of contention, the consequence of which must be unhappy either way; unhappy as a premium on misconduct if the child is successful; thoroughly unhappy if the advantage accrues to the elder, since such advantage can only come through forfeiture of character, individuality, and self-respect on the part of the little delinquent. Perceiving that the older party is the stronger, whatever possibilities for evasion exist in the culprit are sure to be called into active exercise, with their woful train of falsehood, trickery, and hypocrisy.

Then why not, since punishment fails as a motive, fall back upon *rewards?* The reply is, that these are hardly less reprehensible, as the certain result is to engender sordid and self-seeking proponsities. In other words, it is a species of intellectual bribery and corruption. It is not a doing of work for work's sake, but merely for the sake of the pay.

Amid the failure, then, of all these ordinary resorts and practices, upon what incentives can we fall back? Again the answer comes, (through the aid of mental physiology), "upon the general analysis of human emotion." Thus intellectually armed and accoutred to meet the problem, we plainly find that our emotional nature includes two familiar states or conditions of our organism—those of pain and pleasure; the first (pain) ever tending to a diminution of our vital force and its activities, the second (pleasure) ever tending to their stimulation and enhancement. Common sense would, therefore, teach us at the outset that the best results can only be attained when brought into alliance with pleasure as the motive—pleasure, not arbitrarily and unhealthfully conferred, but pleasure flowing naturally from the occupation, and meaning by pleasure an innocent and wholesome enjoyment of life in its more solid and substantial pursuits.

Taking advantage, therefore, of the keen proclivities and eager curiosity which are inherent in the very being of every healthy child, the wise teacher keeps introducing his pupils into ever new surroundings, seeking at the same time to refer them continually to the facts, forms, and items they have previously acquired. Thus, a judgment as to the difference of the freshly perceived facts from those before known, is at once provoked through adequate questionings, while arising doubts are settled by illustrations and researches made by the pupil himself. Thus, at the close of each recitation the scholar has acquired a few new data. He did not obtain these from the teacher directly. He has found them out for himself; and the consciousness and charm of such a creative activity rarely fails to be a sufficient inducement to the child to whet his intellectual appetite and keep it ever keen. This method would serve to illustrate the course successfully adopted in the objective primary department.

In the secondary, more complicated objects would be presented to the pupil, whose trained perceptions would then have gained a sufficient delicacy to familiarize him with very minute discriminations. It is he again who, from his own insight, answers the questions in reference to new subjects, by drawing on his stock of knowledge previously appropriated, the teacher's *role* being only to awaken the attention to relations and sequences as they co-ordinate themselves in increasingly minute details.

As an illustration of this method of self-help, or self-instruction, Mr. von Taube relates the following: The girls in the chemistry class—and I would say right here, that with the exception of certain exercises and occupations in the tool-house and gymnasium, this whole method applies as well to the girls as to the boys—the girls, then, in the chemistry class knew that to obtain the atomic weight of an element it was necessary to reduce it to gas and compare equal volumes of the same with hydrogen. Now, the object was to find out the weight of carbon, a non-evaporable body. The girls asked themselves if there was any gas containing carbon. It was ascertained that numerous such gases existed—for instance, carbonic acid, which experiment proved to consist of two atoms of oxygen and one of carbon. The total weight of the carbonic acid was ascertained to be forty-four times that of an equal volume of hydrogen. The only question put by the teacher was, "What is the weight of a *single* molecule of oxygen?" The class straightway replied, "Sixteen times that of hydrogen." Then one of the little ones, seeing immediately that if one molecule of carbonic acid—being forty-four times as heavy as one molecule of hydrogen—consisted of two parts of oxygen and one of carbon, and that the two molecules of oxygen, sixteen each, must therefore give thirty-two, jumped at the answer, (taking the thirty-two from the forty-four,) and said that the atomic weight of carbon compared to hydrogen was twelve.

This is sufficient to illustrate how a system of self-help, based upon experiment and observation, merely from the pleasure it affords, constitutes the main incentive, which, ever growing and strengthing, through the objective or primary courses, on into the subjective or more elderly courses, leads the pupil ever eagerly forward towards fresh intellectual attainments. Over and over again my own children, while relating at dinner some new fact which they had gained that day, have said, "Oh, it was such jolly fun!"

If, on the other hand, some occasional pupil becomes so refractory that the discipline of pain is needed, I am informed that the moral punishment of sending the transgressor home has been found entirely effectual. Moreover, as a substitute for the scoldings and blows which most boys and girls are subjected to, each pupil is required to keep a school diary, in which is recorded, by their own hand, their good and evil doings both in study and conduct, thus constituting the children themselves as judges unto themselves, and saving a world of rough friction between them and their teachers. Its results have proved in practice to be most beneficial.

"But," I fancy I hear it said, "you have as yet told us nothing about the tool-house." I have purposely reserved this topic for a special description. All of us now know that the kindergarten is an established and recognized department of infant education. I need not, therefore, dwell at length upon it. It is, indeed, in the great kindergarten of nature that every baby must begin its learning in the use of its eyes, ears, nose, and fingers; but later we see how, through the exercises of the kindergarten proper, the little children find it at once a heaven of delight and the widest scope of instruction, as obtained in their games, their mats, their stick houses, their modelings, their geometrical figures, etc., etc., etc. Why, then, I ask, should this most desirable development of a keen perception stop with the *infant?* Is not the boy and girl, from seven to fifteen, just as eager and just as much in need of such development? Our research, indeed, into mental physiology certainly indicates that such facilities *should* be provided.

Frœbel, although the great pioneer, advanced no further in his curriculum than to recommend objective teaching, and as far as his work went, it was, beyond all cavil, a grand one. But the evil was, and is, that the pupil, after having left the kindergarten, ran the risk of losing every advantage he had there gained from the need he then found himself in of continuing his schooling under the antiquated method; and just here it is that manual training, as an essential factor, finds its place. Let us then state, point by point, the advantages of the tool-house as a means of educational enlightenment.

First—Let us look at it from the bread-and-butter standpoint simply, or as a preparation for money-making. Man's life may be defined as having two well-traced ultimate ends, viz.: personal needs and satisfactions, and social needs and satisfactions. As regards personal needs, we may bluntly place the dollar ahead, since it contains within itself the only possibility of material progress, it alone bringing the leisure which leads from savagery to civilization.

It will be remembered that the second requisite of education, which I cited from Herbert Spencer, was to afford the training for what he calls *indirect* self-preservation; that is, the gaining of a knowledge necessary for a livelihood. In this connection, Spencer affirms the truism, that it is with the production and distribution of commodities that men are for the most part occupied, and he then says, that to this end knowledge is power—that is, the physical, chemical, and vital properties of the articles dealt in should be understood; that is, again, physical science should be understood; teaching of the lever, the wheel and the axle; of the steam engine, the safety lamp, the microscope; of the telegraph and telephone; of heat, light and electricity; of bleaching and dyeing; of the reduction of ores; of gas refining; of distilling; of manures; of soils, and so on, through an endless catalogue. For what we call learning a business, really implies learning the *science* involved in it; and since most men are in many businesses, most business men should, as a business precaution, know many sciences. But Spencer, although he dived as deep into the subject as the English erudition of twenty years ago allowed, did not penetrate deep enough. Two steps more were needed to perfect his own scheme, and these were the kindergarten and its direct successor, the tool-house, or manual training-school.

Amid the chances and changes of life, it is impossible for any one to exaggerate how important it may be for a young man to know a trade, and the general tool-house training under consideration should fit him capably not only for one, but for many trades, such as work in wood and metals, plain and ornamental; printing and editing work; work in solders, enamels, lubricants, dyes, and other applications of chemistry; work in connection with mechanical appliances and steam engines; telegraphic and photographic work, etc., etc., all of which can be reduced, on a final analysis, to a few fundamental processes, and can be confined to the use and instrumentality of a limited number of tools.

But I fancy I hear many parents at once entering their demurrer by saying, "I don't want my son or daughter to demean themselves by learning common trades." And this brings me to the next argument in favor of the tool-house, which is:

Second—The growing importance of the trades, or manual training.

The old caste spirit of India, Persia, Egypt, and even Rome and Greece, regulated the trades as bodies apart, and made of the workmen slaves. A cobbler a cobbler had to remain. Even intermarriages between the trades were for a long time interdicted. They had no rights which the aristocracy were bound to respect—the former were the exploiters, the latter the exploited. The inflow of the Northern Teutons helped to democratize the Latin races, but for ages the monk was the only connecting link between the workingmen and the upper classes. Later, for the crusades, money and muscles were needed. The trades supplied them, and towards the close of the middle age, the craft guilds arose. These began to accumulate wealth enough to engage in business operations for themselves. But it required the brewer, Cromwell of England, and the Reign of Terror in France, to prove to the world that the *poletariat* were possessed of the same senses and feelings as those of the hitherto more privileged classes, and consequently entitled to the same rights of existence and enjoyment. As an illustration of this, the constitution of Poland of 1793 contained the then radical and revolutionary affirmation that every peasant is as much a man as the nobleman above him, to say nothing of our own Declaration of Independence, which affirms the immortal averment that all men are created equal, and endowed with the same inalienable rights to life, liberty, and the pursuit of happiness. Although a growing humanitarianism has had much to do with this movement of industrial emancipation, it must also be recognized that the advancing commercial and political importance of the trades, as trades, has also exerted a vast and mighty influence; and, perhaps, the time is not far distant when mankind will accord to them the meed they so richly deserve, as being among the truest promoters and benefactors of civilization.

Thus it has at last come about that in the Russian public schools the learning of a trade is made obligatory; and throughout Europe polytechnic institutes, with courses of manual training, have become required parts of education. But notwithstanding such innovations, the predominance of the old caste spirit in Europe is still so strong, that of few Europeans in good standing can it be said (as it readily might of many Americans) that he started in life with a tool in his hand; and it requires no spirit of prophecy to foretell that the dandy who despises tools will have to make way before the man who can master them, just as the poetical Indian is fast disappearing before the champions of the ax, the engine, and the rail. It seems, therefore, as if it were chiefly in America that manual training can be much hoped for as an effectual educational adjunct, without the risk of stumbling against "good form" and the daintiness of a *dillètante* culture. It is only America which, having subordinated war to industry, can emblazon upon its flag the inspiring motto, "*Le travail ennoblit*"—"Work ennobles."

But trusting that this short historical sketch has been sufficient to show to us the growing importance of the great common people, with their great common trades, it may be rejoined that the college student at seventeen or eighteen years of age can follow these callings, through the facilities which are being admirably supplied by many of our institutions (for instance, Cornell University and the College of the City of New York). But, again, our mental physiology must be recalled. Propose such a student, for instance, as apprentice to a carpenter, blacksmith, printer, or mechanician of any kind. They would bluntly laugh, and say: "You can't expect me to do anything with him, now that he is nearly a man. He can never learn my trade. His fingers are already clumsy. His eye is no longer capable of seizing the distinction of one thirty-second of an inch in length, thickness or inclination. It would simply be loss of time to both of us You had best reserve him for the counting-house, where he belongs." And the mechanician would be right. As our mental physiology has shown, the time for training the young man's perceptions had already passed by. We thus can see how, between the kindergarten and the actual trade, the tool-house stands as an essential intermediary, since it represents a track or channel which can only be traveled or passed over at a fixed stage of our existence. If we attempt to retrace our steps (in manual training, as well as in other branches,) at eighteen or twenty years of age, we only do so to find that it is too late, and to read on the tablet of a lost opportunity the words, the ever sad words—"It might have been." The manual training in the colleges may be of enormous value as far as experimental knowledge is concerned, but never can it supply the need of a course obtained in younger days, at the appropriate age, when the senses are all aglow and eager for the work.

Third—*The tool-house, as a means for the application of knowledge.* With all said, it is not as an end, but as a means towards an end, that manual training is most valuable. Hitherto, we have been speaking of such manual training as a mere instrumentality to teach a trade, the trade itself, as a calling, being the sole object and end in view; but the tool-house must now be considered in the light of a channel or agency (and, in fact, the only one) through which to *apply*, and thus to *realize*, what would otherwise be merely theoretical knowledge. In this aspect it becomes magnified into an unspeakably enhanced importance.

It has already been made evident that knowledge implies not only perception and memory, but also the individual and personal *grasp* of facts through practical application. Thus, the study of the natural sciences, unless supplemented by a conjoint training of the hand and mind, remains doubtful in its results and tedious in its acquisition. In truth, knowledge unapplied can hardly be called knowledge at all. Our frail human nature labors under the fundamental necessity of working out, and thus of practicalizing, its conceptions and ideas. The intimation of this is observable in the case of every child, who, at the earliest age, endeavors to find out for himself all the purposes possible to which any kind of material can be applied. Our mental analysis explains the rationale of this tendency, and the truth is that no school method yet adopted fully provides for the thorough digestion of the facts and items which have been intellectually provided. Such facts and items, unless applied, remain only so many unused arms in the arsenal of the mind, too rusty for use when the need of them arises; whereas a proper course of manual training not only keeps the facts fresh in the memory, but also serves as an early initiation into that invaluable mental capacity, which we call *constructive genius or faculty.* As an illustration, let us resort to the abstract ideas of space, time, and number, which are divisions of primary importance.

The whole of mathematics and mechanics are nothing but the development of our perceptions in these regards. For these sciences are, on final analysis, seen to be based on our early experience with concrete matter; and even in the simplest of their formulas they represent to us generalizations founded on facts. (Let us remember, in this connection, that humanity progresses because able to assimilate and profit by the knowledge of the past. Therefore an everlasting justice seems to decree that unless we sow we shall not reap, and that in order to reap, our individual mentality, like that of the race, must pass through the whole process of sense-acquisition—coming thus, and thus alone, to permanent perceptions, not by means of abstractions and rote-learning, but through the impressions produced by objects.) Thus a carpenter, or mechanic of almost any kind, will know his tables of denominate numbers better than will the student who may have solved hundreds of examples, and the practical draughtsman will be quicker to detect the error of the sixteenth of an inch than will the theoretical learner of all the geometries. Turning to mechanics for another illustration, many adults will even yet remember how puzzling it was to solve the problems of the three levers; and yet a few simple constructions drawn—or, better yet, wrought out in wood—by the pupil himself, will stamp the theory in a manner never to be forgotten.

Furthermore, mathematics represents abstracts; abstracts are merely mental symbols of the concrete; they are used only for the purposes of the concrete; the concrete always remains as of primary importance, and therefore, unless we wish to waste our children's powers on empty puzzles, we must recognize the principal value of mathematics as consisting in its application. And as time goes on, this method supplies more and more of the minutiæ both of mathematics and mechanics to the interested learner, and its chief, though subsequent advantage, ere long becomes manifest, viz.: in the development of an abstract and dispassionate judgment, thus imparting a wider and more philosophical capacity, till it at last eventuates that even the intrigues of courts, the strength or feeblenesss of human nature, the good and evil passions, and individual interests, become to the constructive statesman, as it were, so many mechanical energies, every one of them representable by its numerical exponent, and of value to him only as he may be enabled to separate or combine them. So it finally results that by graduated steps we are led on further and further, till, through the composition and resolution of mechanical forces, we are enabled to face, and as far as may be, to solve, the deep enigmas of humanity, whether approached from the standpoint of the preacher, the poet, the politico-economist, or the philanthropist. In all these cases intellectual constructiveness is the true basis of their operations. And in this aspect let the commonplace objection be no longer flung against this method, viz.: that its materiality is deadening to the imagination. I affirm that it does not slay imagination; it merely regulates it. Imagination may be called the faculty of reconstructing new combinations from old perceptions. If, hitherto, the words and phrases of dead languages have been found to foster the fancy, how much more may this not be the case hereafter from handling *facts* in every field, through all the realms of nature and of life? Imagination, then, no longer playing like a *feu follet*, but linked to everlasting law, will henceforth lead us on, not to deceive, but to instruct, inspire and elevate. And so, finally, the school, which can by its method impart to the highest average possible, and in the easiest way possible, the greatest constructive imaginative power, must become the school of the future. And this, it is claimed, the tool-house should accomplish.

Fourth.—The Tool-house in its Moral Influence.

I here also cover the third leading theme of my paper, which is moral education in general. Astonishing as the training which I have been describing is in its intellectual results, these really grow dim before its moral effects. Morality may be simply defined as the science and art of right living. Let us first touch upon it as a science, though, in connection with the tool-house, it is upon it as an art that I wish particularly to dwell.

Glancing at it as a science, in the first place, a certain morality may be said to exist in the mere investigation of facts as facts, whether they be phenomena of the organic or of the inorganic world, and everywhere throughout this whole school-system the child is brought face to face with the great truthfulness of nature—the great truthfulness of fact. Emerson has magnificently said: "Day creeps after day, each full of facts—dull, strange, despised things, that we cannot, at first, enough despise—which we call heavy, prosaic and desert . . . . and presently the aroused intellect finds gold and gems in one of these scorned facts; then finds that the day of facts is a rock of diamonds—that a fact is an Epiphany of God." The Bible well says: "As a man thinketh, so is he." If he thinks truth, he is apt to become truthful. Thus it is that the stars sing to the child the truth of their orbits; the rocks relate the truth of their strata; the flowers assert the truth of their structure. So, truth in the organic and inorganic world faces the learner at every step.

But, be it allowed, morality proper, as a science, pertains not to dead matter, but to life itself in its human relationships and motives. To this, therefore, for a moment, we turn.

Morality as a science, I have just said, is the science of right living. Its object is to provide a mental guide for the activities and duties of life. In alluding, in a previous part of my essay, to the incentives which should actuate the children, viz.: pleasure and pain, moral causes and effects have necessarily been hinted at, but they need to be enlarged upon. In the nursery, then, and in the school, as, indeed, in the world at large, that alone seems to be the truly salutary discipline which visits upon all conduct, good and bad, the pleasurable or painful consequences which, in the nature of things, such conduct tends to produce. Moral cause and consequence is, therefore, the chief thing to be inculcated—good actions leading to good consequences, bad actions to bad consequences. The school-system, in other words, must be one of pure justice. In accordance with the old adage, that "the burnt child dreads the fire," the learner must discover, through teaching and experience, that "whatsoever he soweth that shall he also reap," and, furthermore, that "the way of the transgressor is hard." But such rude experience is often not only a *hard* but a *hardening* master. While pain and pleasure, felt as consequences, may lie at the root of morality as a science, it must be remembered that this same morality is not only a science, but an art as well. True, the art must wait upon the science, but it must also supplement it in the shape of practice. So let us now pass on to morality as an art. Morality under this view becomes nothing more than habits taken in the right direction. "Habit," the old adage well says, "becomes a second nature." If the intellectual discernment of consequences, as following causes, represents the *science*, the *art* may be defined as the habit of avoiding the bad and cultivating the good consequence; and the young can best reach the *science* through the art, and the practice of the art. Here, as in other fields, there is no expediency in teaching the abstract instead of the concrete. To begin with the definitions or rules in moral instruction (as has always been the old-fashioned way) before having cultivated the practice, would be to make the same mistake as to start in grammar with the laws of syntax before having inculcated the signification of the parts of speech.

"Just as the twig is bent the tree's inclined," and the lesson of the practical art of ethics is, that if some evil proclivities need to be eradicated, the best way is to stifle them by means of good predispositions substituted, through consistent examples set and steady habits formed. And just here it is that the ethical power of the tool-house manifests itself. For if what I have given is a true exposition of morality, then it is at once evident what immense power manual training, as a part of education, may exert in the formation of character. The mere habit of organized recreation afforded by the tool-house is of itself an enormous aid. It is an unspeakable gain, even if a negative one, to keep boys out of mischief. You often must have noticed how youngsters love just to watch work, such as blacksmithing, housebuilding, or the like. How much more, then, do they not become enchanted and enthused over some machine or model which they seek to fashion for themselves, even though it be empirically and rudely formed.

Under a proper curriculum of manual training, these inherent youthful impulses are taken hold of and so systematized that the otherwise idle and refractory youngster is kept continuously and absorbingly occupied.

One of the inevitable effects resulting from the old, rigorous discipline of the antiquated school, as, indeed, of the home, was to make both school and home hateful; the necessary reaction from which was to drive the pupil to seek his pleasure in mere pleasure-seeking. Not to find his joy in his work, but to find his joy in vapid fun, became his chief end of life. Hence, for want of school and homemade recreative, recreation was necessarily found in sky-larking and mischief-making, in a penny's worth of vicious hilarity gained to-day at the expense of a dollar's worth of character sacrificed to-morrow. How many a wayward and rebellious boy, ungovernable by the old tutorial and parental methods, might not have been saved, if taken at a sufficiently early age, by this new, judicious, and beneficent system—a system which provides materials for the hand and head to act upon, as naturally as the digestive organs assimilate appropriate food!

Busy fingers and busy heads leave little room for vice, and work, directed in wholesome channels and motived by curiosity and gratified inquiry, builds up character unconsciously and almost automatically. The pupil finds himself, in this way, continuously overcoming difficulties by his own personal effort, and therefore finds himself gaining that most invaluable of moral stimulations, the feeling of self-reliance.

It is an old saying, that "where there is a will there is a way." But how true, also, is the opposite, that there is often a will where there is no way open to it. To present a way, through the provision of adequate facilities, and so to bring the will and the way both into continual partnership, such is one of the great offices of the tool-house, leading to the habit of self-reliance just spoken of. But further, the pupil is, all this while, acquiring a continual insight into the most important facts which relate to the productive activity of the earth. So, widening his scope of existence by the popular nature of his employment, he is necessarily led into a close moral sympathy with the wants, needs, and difficulties of the workmen of the world. Moreover, when the tool-house shall be fully organized, it is the intention of the management, in connection with a proper supervision, to introduce a democratic method of administration (self-government) among the pupils, as far as the same is feasible. They are each to be the owner of one or more shares of stock, with the right to draw its accruing dividends, thus imparting a financial interest in the concern; the boys are to elect their own foreman in each department; they are to manufacture their own products, and sell them in open market; they are to keep their own books, and under due bounds, and by means of meetings and debate in open caucus, to regulate their own order and discipline. This school, therefore, instead of being something apart from the great run of common life, becomes incorporated with it, and no violent break is felt when the student-career merges naturally and almost unconsciously into political, business or professional existence.

The pupil's experience and love for the smaller republic of the school now becomes extended subjectively to the larger republic of country. He realizes that outside of him is the great social organism. In his own needs he sees the basis of his rights—in the needs of others the basis of his duties. The feeling of losses and gains to himself is applied in imagination unto others. Their losses and gains become a part of his own being. In their happiness he comes to seek his own. The knowledge of rights and the feelings of duty widen, till finally the moral keynote is reached in the adaptation of his life to a wide, harmonious scale, where love, thought and act combine and culminate in a lofty æsthetic and human enthusiasm.

Perhaps I may profitably pause right here, for a moment, as I approach the end of my essay, to say, by way of parenthesis, that this school-system, taken in its totality, presents to my mind a complete reconciliation between the antagonistic positions of Drs. Eliot and McCosh, (Presidents respectively of Harvard and Princeton Colleges) in their debate before the Nineteenth Century Club, on the "Elective versus the Enforced System of Study and Behavior." The former asserted that in a University a student from eighteen years of age should select his own studies and govern himself, while the latter claimed that this would end in the choice of easy and one-sided courses, and also in looseness of deportment. Each of these academic giants seemed to me to represent a great idea in education. Dr. McCosh properly insisted upon the need of a general culture in literature, language, science and philosophy, while Dr. Eliot's apparently irreconcilable attitude was equally sound, to wit.: that after eighteen it was profoundly inexpedient to subject the scholar to any undue surveillance. What I affirm is, (and my affirmation is founded on a hint given in Dr. Eliot's paper) that at the age spoken of any youth of average intelligence, educated under the method I am advocating, with its democratic form of administration, will have received not only a groundwork of liberal culture amply sufficient to enable him—under the advice of teachers and parents—to choose his own special line of collegiate application, but I maintain, also, that the preparation which the school ensures in the way of self-government should be a guarantee of his ability to oversee and regulate his own conduct. And furthermore, be it emphatically understood, an immense and invaluable practical result would be that several of the most important years of life would thuswise be saved, since the student, having finished his general training at eighteen, could make himself ready for his business or profession by twenty-one, the average age at which mere graduation from our colleges now ordinarily takes place.

Returning from this détour, I would add right here, as my concluding point, that the Gramercy Park School does not profess to be, in the strict and technical sense of the term, a religious academy. As it would be impossible to please all sects, sectarianism is rigidly excluded, and the school is very wisely organized as a purely secular one: Denominational instruction is left, and properly left, to the parents and the home.

But if a secular, in no sense can the school be called an irreligious one. As Mr. von Taube eloquently says: "a fully developed and educated mind cannot possibly be irreligious, in the higher acceptation of the word."

A prominent city clergyman kindly provides me with the following quotation from one of his sermons: "A divine order, could it be known and its laws obeyed, would end the disorders of earth. This divine order lies not behind man, but before him. The realization of this order is the aim of the *education* of man. The realization of this order is to begin from within and work outward. It is to be first a work of personal reform and then a work of social reform. The realization of this order is actually taking place in the world. The Kingdom of God is at hand, brought ever nigh to man, through the work of His spirit in society, capable in a time, brief to the vision of the seer, of coming down upon the earth. When this order is established, it will be the reign of God manifested in Jesus."

A philosopher, decried by many as unduly heterodox, has thus also defined religion: "Religion is the tie by which man's feelings and thoughts within, and his actions without, are co-ordinated into health and harmony with each other, with society and the world, with the past and the future."

I give these definitions of religion, both according to the clergyman and the positivist. Under either view, the divine or the human—both are in reality one—this school, though it calls itself only secular, is, in reality, in the deep meaning of the word, a religious institution. It seeks to effect the harmonious union of the hand with the head, and the head with the heart. Based on liberty, it would place that liberty under law, and consecrate the whole being to the highest humanity.

Miss Haines, the celebrated predecessor of Mr. von Taube, was the practical founder of the Kindergarten in America. From the model she established it worked its way into its present large acceptance.

The Tool-house is its legitimate successor, and ought as such to be supported by the intelligence of this metropolis, in order that it, likewise, may become a good seed planted to bring forth fruit a hundred fold, in the physical, intellectual, industrial and moral education of the youth of our land.

www.ingramcontent.com/pod-product-compliance
Lightning Source LLC
LaVergne TN
LVHW011139110826
845150LV00008B/2417

* 9 7 8 1 4 1 8 1 9 3 5 6 0 *